TEACHING YOUNG CHILDREN
TO CARE:

DEVELOPING SELF-ESTEEM

Teaching Young Children to Care

37 Activities for Developing
SELF-ESTEEM

Dorothy Dixon

TWENTY-THIRD PUBLICATIONS
Mystic, Connecticut

Revised edition 1990

Twenty-Third Publications
P.O. Box 180
185 Willow Street
Mystic, CT 06355
(203) 536-2611

ISBN 0-89622-436-8
Library of Congress Catalog Card Number 90-70418

Contents

Attitude Sessions

Accomplishment Sessions

Introduction

Education is usually described as promoting growth in three areas: cognitive, affective, and psychomotor. *Teaching Young Children to Care: 37 Activities for Developing Self-Esteem* (there is a companion volume, *Teaching Young Children to Care: 37 Activities for Developing Concern for Others*) is a program of affective education. As such, it promotes and enhances children's attitudes, interests, motivations, care, and concern about all that is happening in their lives. It was designed for use in early childhood classrooms from kindergarten through grade three, in public, private, and parochial schools. It is also intended for use in programs of child nurture in parish schools of religious education and summer Bible programs.

The Felt Need
In a world that is steadily growing more technological and less personal, there is urgent need for better ways of bringing persons into meaningful relationships with one another. The growing alienation among students in many schools in this country alerts educators to the need for programs that build personhood in an atmosphere of caring. As the high incidence of family breakups grows, and the mobility of families from one location to another continues to be common practice, the need for regular, dependable group experiences and guided conversations for small children becomes even more obvious. It is out of these realizations that *Teaching Young Children to Care: 37 Activities for Developing Self-Esteem* has been developed. It was written out of a felt need.

The sessions are broadly graded; each can be used, with thoughtful modification, with children from kindergarten through grade three. Enough session plans are offered to allow teachers to choose the topics best suited to the situations in their classrooms. For each session there should be an adult leader and a group of children, preferably sitting in a circle.

Caring Circles
These circles are called *caring circles*. Children need to feel a sense of belonging to a consistently-meeting group, and the idea of having their own "club" is appealing. The emphasis in the caring club is on belonging together and sharing

ideas in such a way that each child gets to know himself or herself fully, and also gets to know peers in a way that is more than casual. Beyond getting to know themselves, the children in the caring circles grow in three specific ways: in self-esteem, in empathy, and in caring behavior. *Teaching Young Children to Care: 37 Activities for Developing Self-Esteem* provides 37 sessions to deal with the first of these areas, self-esteem. These include topics aimed at awareness of one's feelings, wonder at oneself and nature generally, and a sense of accomplishment —all to foster self-esteem.

Each teacher will find his or her own best way for grouping the children into the circles. If the class size is small enough, up to a dozen children, the whole class can get into a caring circle. But if the class is larger than that, it should be divided in half, or, if it contains close to thirty children, it should be divided three ways. Heterogeneous grouping is recommended, although one first-grade teacher used her reading groups for caring circles and found that the plan worked well since she already had the group assembled. Each session can be repeated in successive years, because the conversation of each child will differ from year to year, making the experience new even though the basic session plan remains the same.

While a teacher may simply select topics as required, this program is best used in the sequence in which it is given here.

Circle Environment

One difference in arrangement between caring circles and other children's work groups is that there is no need for a table. Caring circles work best when participants are either in small chairs, or sitting on the floor in a circle. One group made "sit upons" from linoleum squares laced together, with a thickness of newspapers in between. Another group used carpet squares from store samples for sitting cushions. It is important that each child have a designated space so that there be no confusion at circle time.

Early in the program, provision is made for some ground rules so that every child is guaranteed a chance to speak and to be heard by every circle member. The teacher or other adult leader becomes the facilitator to maximize the effectiveness of each session.

Schedule

The classroom teacher may well be wondering how the caring circles can be worked into a weekly schedule. There are a number of ways. If the class is to be divided because of its size, perhaps an aide, parent, or school counselor could take one caring circle while the teacher takes the other. But if an additional person is not available, one group could meet with the teacher while the other children work at learning centers or do paper work at their tables or desks.

It is recommended that each caring club meet at least twice a week. A session is designed to last about twenty minutes, but the teacher should judge, each in his or her own circumstances, whether it is profitable to prolong or abbreviate the session. Suggestions are made after most lessons to enable the teacher to extend the session.

If the administrator or teacher asks, "How can I afford time for this program?" the better question might well be, "Can I afford not to have a strong program of affective education in my classroom (or school)?" The attitudes that the children will develop in their caring circles will permeate the rest of the week. Children who understand who they are and are motivated by a sense of purposefulness will achieve more in the long run than children who are kept "at the grindstone" day in and day out and do not learn self-esteem and a caring attitude.

Developing Attitudes

Classroom conflict is minimized in rooms where children have learned to care about themselves and others. When conflicts do occur, children who have participated in caring circles are better able to resolve differences because they have developed these attitudes and the use of language to express their feelings.

Caring circle time is more than a time set apart for discussion and activities; it should influence a whole way of life permeating the classroom atmosphere and the children's activities all during their waking hours. Parents should be informed of the program, for they will notice its effects at home as well as in school. In fact, they might be encouraged to have caring circles among members of the household at regular intervals. It would be good to have at least one organization meeting for parents and teachers devoted to introducing *Teaching Young Children to Care: 37 Activities for Developing Self-Esteem.*

"Positive Regard"

Caring circles must be occasions in which each child is viewed, in the words of Dr. Carl Rogers, with "unconditional positive regard." The attitude of the adult leader of the circles needs to be one of genuine acceptance of the children and their feelings. Positive comments such as, "That really was a happy feeling, wasn't it!" or "Thank you, Karen; you really gave us a good example!" should abound at circle time.

The adult leader will keep the conversation flowing on the topic of the day, but even deviant remarks should be met with positive suggestions. For instance, the leader can meet a particular remark with a comment such as, "Oh, that's interesting, Harry. We can talk about it later, but right now our topic is...."

Children should be encouraged to help in the recapitulation of each circle meeting. One helper each session can summarize what each child has said, so that everyone in the caring circle knows that he or she has been heard. There should be both an enthusiasm and a tenderness in all the conversations. Each member of the circle should leave the group feeling an emotional warmth and an anticipation for the next meeting.

An important result of this program is the language development that occurs as the children speak on the circle topics. This program is designed to maximize each child's input. Topics are structured enough to promote interest, but unstructured enough to give children a chance to use initiative in their responses. Shy children have been observed to speak in longer than usual sentences in caring circles because they grew accustomed to the group and felt safe in offering their conversation.

Self-Esteem Sessions

These sessions are designed to start children in the ways of group membership, to develop awareness of one's own feelings, to increase the sense of awe and wonder, and to enhance the feeling of "I-can-ness." This is the long and careful path toward the nurture of self-esteem in a child. Psychologists tell us that unless a person can value himself or herself, that person cannot value someone else. Children who do not value themselves tend to project their own self-dissatisfaction on others, and engage in constant criticism.

Awareness Sessions

The many sessions on topics related to happy feelings are to sharpen awareness of feelings. Children need to know about their own feelings and to be able to talk about them. Feelings are an integral part of every human being, yet they are not readily visible like hands and feet. Therefore they must be discussed to be understood. Without discussion, feelings can be quite nebulous and even perplexing to small children. We begin our study of feelings with many topics pertaining to happy feelings, since those are the easiest to express, but we move on to other feelings such as sadness, anger, fear, jealousy, and humor.

When children hear their peers tell of experiences that generated each of these feelings, they realize that all feelings are a normal part of being human. Self-awareness, then, instills a positive assurance for the children. Without such assurance, many children feel "odd" or even guilty about feelings that are actually universal.

Attitude Sessions

Attitude, or wonder, sessions are designed to help the children keep alive their inborn response in delight for the created world. In *A Sense of Wonder*, Rachel Carson writes: "If a child is to keep alive his inborn sense of wonder…he needs the companionship of at least one adult who can share it, rediscovering with him the mystery of the world we live in."

For this reason, *Teaching Young Children to Care: 37 Activities for Developing Self-Esteem* contains many experiences in which the sense of wonder in each child is enhanced, and the child feels fully alive, and really "turned on" to life. To be able to live with enthusiasm is a gift we wish to nurture in each of our children. By nurturing the "fully alive" feeling, we help counteract not only apathy but also escapism.

Accomplishment Sessions

The final sessions of this program have to do with achievement or the good feeling of accomplishment. They are designed to encourage the children to talk about things they can do at home and at school. In talking about these feats, the children realize in a very specific way their own self-worth. Caution: Achievements *enhance* a sense of self-worth. Do not give the impression that the lack of achievements means the absence of self-worth. Each child has fundamental value as a human, regardless of his or her particular achievements.

Thus out of discussions on feelings, wonder, and accomplishments, the children grow in positive self-concepts and thereby enhance their self-esteem. Moving through the topics in this section, the children get in touch with their inner selves and the deep inner wellsprings from which they move. In a sense, each child is answering the prime question "Who am I?" in an affirmative manner. Each child is realizing, "I am somebody with a name, a wide range of feelings in a wondrous world, and I am learning to do many things quite well! I care about myself." A valuable by-product of the enhanced self-esteem is the increased academic motivation and achievement that follows.

Teaching Young Children to Care: 37 Activities for Developing Self-Esteem not only develops positive self-regard but also indirectly enhances the achievement level of the students in the schools. The time spent in this program is not at the expense of basic education, but rather is an asset to the total curriculum.

In addition to this program on developing self-esteem in kindergarden to third-grade children, there is a companion program to develop in these same children a concern for others: *Teaching Young Children to Care: 37 Activities for Developing Concern for Others.*

The Name Game

Objective

To enable the children to say the full name of each child in the group, and to help them to decide which name to use for each child, according to that child's preference

Materials

Bean bags, name tags: "My name is _____ and I like _____."

Procedure

Gather the children into a circle and explain that this meeting is the beginning of many times they will be together. Help them feel that this is a special time together. Suggest that they can call the group "Our Caring Club." During these times together, they belong to it as friends of one another. Mention that the first part of friendship is knowing one another's names.

Greet each child by name. This reinforces awareness of the importance of names. The greeting can be as simple as "Good morning, Sandy. Good morning, Paul. Good morning, Sarah." Then ask others if they want to greet each child by name in a similar way. Usually the children will be eager for a turn.

Follow this by a name game. With some groups, the most appropriate game is a simple bean bag toss. With a bean bag in your hand, explain that you will say a name and toss the bag. The person whose name is called is to catch the bag, then call another name and toss the bag again. This provides some activity (while seated) and reinforces the remembrance of each child's name.

With second- or third-grade children, the game could be a more complex one. For instance, the children could play "My name is Peter and I like peanuts." The next child would say, "His name is Peter and he likes peanuts, and my name is Debbie and I like doughnuts." Each child in turn would try to say the previous names and likes, and add his or her own name and likes to the list. The "like" should be an alliteration of the child's own name. Of course, the last few children will have many names to remember and perhaps persons from the group can help them remember. Or if name tags are made, they can read them.

There could follow a discussion of middle and last names, and even nicknames. The thrust of the session is to acquaint the children and to build a group spirit. The art of listening to one another should also grow from an experience of this kind. If several children have the same first name, find a way to distinguish each child.

Talk about how it feels to have someone call you by name. When a friend says, "Hello, Suzi," does that greeting mean more to Suzi than just plain "Hello"? What happens when we introduce two persons to each other? Could we introduce them if we did not know their names? What can we do to find out a person's name if we do not know it? Can we ask which name a person prefers if that person has more than one name?

If time permits, you could go into the meaning of names. A name list with meanings can usually be obtained from any library or in dictionaries.

The dismissal should come quickly when the children begin to get restless. But end with a flourish, with words such as, "We have really learned a lot about ourselves and our names today. Thank you for coming to our club meeting, and we'll meet again on ... (give day of the week)."

As the children are dismissed, suggest that they ask their parents how and why they selected the names they gave their children. These accounts can be related at the next session.

Lesson Extender
An important extension of this session would be a discussion of what to do if two children have the same name. Comment in an interested (not a distressed) way that it happens often that two or more children in a classroom will have the same name. List all the ways in which these two (or more) children of the same name are different. Decide how to distinguish them, either by adding the initial of the last name, or using a nickname for one and a full name for the other. Agree that the persons are very individual even though the names are similar.

Have the children design name tags. To do this, give each child a paper about 8 1/2" x 11". Have each child print his or her name in large letters about two inches high, lengthwise on the paper, in the center. Let them use first names only. For preschool children, you may need to letter each child's name for the child. Then have the children make a design around their names. They can just color the paper with crayons, or they can paste pictures on the paper that show items or activities special to each child. More advanced children could draw pictures of themselves, or activities they like. They could include family members, or their family pet, or both.

The name tags could be placed on a bulletin board, or the children could wear their name tags for the caring sessions, by affixing them to their chests with an adhesive.

૨

Making Our Club Rules

Objective

To help children learn the concept of rule-making by making some rules so that the circle sessions will go smoothly

Materials

A large sheet of paper on a flip chart or stand, a wide felt marker

Procedure

Gather the children in a circle and have the flip chart and felt marker handy. Ask the children if they learned anything about how they were named. Call upon them one at a time to tell the group what they learned.

Then suggest that since the group is going to be meeting regularly, they will need to make some rules for the "club" so that they can enjoy being together. Ask for suggestions for a plan; listen to each person who speaks, and let everybody get a turn to speak at least once.

As the children make suggestions, accept their ideas warmheartedly, and write them on the flip chart. If the children give negative rules, suggest that they rephrase them in a positive way. For instance, if the children say, "Don't all talk at once," suggest that we can say the same rule positively by stating, "Speak one at a time." Rules should cover the following general approaches: "Speak one at a time." "Raise your hand before speaking." "Listen carefully to others." "Keep arms and legs quiet." Now, cover the flip chart and ask the children to "keep the rules" while they tell the rules, one at a time. Pretend that a new child came into the group and wanted to know the "club rules."

Another idea that should be offered at this time is the plan to summarize each meeting. Ask for a helper to say in a few sentences what was said each session. You can choose a different helper each session, but the plan of summarizing each time needs to be written in the rules.

Lesson Extender

To develop this session further, pick out the five best rules from the list that the children gave, and have the children print them prominently for permanent display in the classroom. Or have each child make an individual chart of the rules, neatly printed, to place inside his or her desk. If the school uses desks that open upward, the list could be taped to the inside of the top surface. In this way the rules are displayed whenever the child opens his or her desk.

Second or third graders could write sentences telling why each rule is important. Younger children could make up songs about rules, or sing the following song, to the tune of "The Farmer in the Dell":

We like to go to school,
We like to know the rule,
Hi-ho it's good to know
The way to act in school.

We help each other know
The way it's good to grow.
Hi-ho it's good to go
To school to learn the rule.

ૐ

A Few of My Favorite Things

Objective
To encourage the children to see themselves as unique individuals by listing their "favorite things to do" and to see the other children as unique persons in the lists they make

Materials
Pencils, paper, pictures of persons engaging in sports, arts, music, reading, playing

Procedure
Let the children look at the pictures for a while. Then if they can write, let each child make a list of ten things he or she especially likes to do. If the children are too young to write, have them each tell one "favorite thing." List these ideas on large sheets of paper, putting the child's name beside each item. Then re-capitulate by re-reading the list for the children to hear.

If the children have made their own lists, it would be good to put the lists in a box, without names on the lists. Then let the children take turns drawing a list from the box and guessing who wrote the list. The children can get to know each child quite well by recognizing his of her likes and by seeing what each person values in activities.

If time permits, return the lists to their original owners, and have the children check the three most favorite items. The mood of the experience should be one of enthusiasm for certain activities, to nurture the "fully alive" feeling in the children, and to help them care about themselves and others as unique human beings.

Lesson Extender
"Favorite things" is a topic that can be explored in many ways, and a topic that

enables each child to establish values and a sense of personal identity and uniqueness. One of the best ways of developing the topic is to have each child make a booklet of "favorite things." Each child could make a montage of pictures pasted to pages, according to his or her selection, and stapled together with a title page. Or the children could draw pictures of themselves doing their "favorite things," and write sentences about their special likes. Some children could even write about their hobbies or their dreams of what they want to be when they grow up. All these creative endeavors could be included in their booklets.

Then have the children learn to sing "These Are a Few of My Favorite Things," a song from the score of the movie and play, *The Sound of Music.* You could get a record of the song from a library, or have the music teacher come in to play the song and lead the singing.

ૐ

Favorite Foods

Objective

To foster in the children an awareness of happy feeling by their describing of favorite foods as dry or juicy, soft or crunchy, sweet or sour, etc. They will also increase in their ability to use adjectives.

Materials

Food pictures, easily obtained from magazines, mounted on construction paper

Procedure

Gather the children into the circle and explain that the foods we eat help to make us who we are. Show pictures of foods. Then ask the children one at a time to volunteer to describe a food they especially like to eat. Let the other children guess what food is being described. It can be a food pictured for the group, or a food shown on a poster. If you have mounted pictures of foods individually, the children can each choose a picture and hold it facing themselves as they describe it. When someone correctly names the food, the child describing it can then turn the picture around so all can see.

Talk about how good it feels to have a full "tummy," and express concern for persons in the world who do not get enough to eat. Let the children tell of any times when they have shared food with others.

Have one child help summarize by telling the favorite food of each child in the circle. Express appreciation for the way the children cooperated in this session on "favorite foods."

Lesson Extender

To develop this session further, lead the children into a discussion of healthy foods and the food groups. Have a chart, or put on the board, the four food groups:

1) Fruits and vegetables,
2) bread and cereal,
3) milk and dairy products,
4) meat.

Discuss the need for some foods from each group each day. Then contrast healthy foods with junk foods. "Junk foods are the kind of treats that have a lot of sugar and little food value."

For preschool and kindergarten children, you could have an assortment of food pictures from magazines, and have the children sort the pictures into two piles: healthy foods and junk foods. A good accompaniment to the lesson would be a "tasting session" whereby the children have snacks of healthy foods such as apple slices or carrot and celery sticks. A "dip" or cream cheese would be good with the snacks. Or you could have the children spread peanut butter on graham crackers.

Children in grades 1-3 could make a list of specific foods and the food groups to which they belong. They could make their lists individually or in small groups. They could print the lists on large paper for bulletin board display if they are working in groups. If they are working individually, they could decorate a chart of food groups for their own kitchens at home. Charts could be made on 12" x 18" sheets with pictures of some of the foods drawn or pasted on the charts.

ॐ

Toy Topics

Objective
To foster the children's growth in awareness of happy feeling as they select and tell about pictures of toys that make them happy

Materials
Pictures of familiar toys cut from catalogues or ads mounted on construction paper. Have at least enough pictures for each child to select one, with several extra. Do not include pictures of toy guns.

Procedure
When the children are seated in the circle, explain that they are going to talk about happy feelings. To do so, each will have a turn to select a picture of a toy and tell how it could give us a happy feeling. Then place the pictures face up on the floor in the center of the circle and allow a minute for the children to look them over. Then ask the children, one at a time, to lift up a picture of a toy and tell why it might make us feel happy. A picture can be used more than once.

The children take turns, at random, talking about the pictures, in the manner of a "show and tell" session. When all who wish have had a turn, ask one child to help you remember what each child has said.

If the children go further into the subject, by telling of toys they have at home, your session is enriched. Invite spontaneous conversation, but remember to stop the session before the interest is worn out. About fifteen minutes is enough. After that time, conclude with a summary such as:

There are many things in our world that give us happy feelings, and sometimes just a stick or a rock can be a great toy when we use our imaginations. Between now and our next meeting, let's think to ourselves about all the things we see at school and home that give us happy feelings. Thank you, boys and girls. We'll meet again on _____.

The goal of the session is for children to realize the happy feelings that come from engaging in play, and the way certain toys enhance the play experience. The final discussion might center on the qualities of good toys: durability, safety, and room for imagination. Toys that are too "ready-made," such as wind-up toys, tend to rob the child of the chance to innovate, imagine, and create. Simple, multi-use toys can be more satisfactory in the long run. Home-made toys can be especially meaningful.

Lesson Extender

To extend this session for preschool and kindergarten children, let them choose toys or sets of blocks from around the room and have a play period of about fifteen minutes. Then gather the group to talk about the feelings they had while engaged in playing with toys.

Children in grades 1-3 could draw pictures of toys they enjoy, or would wish to have. Let them even "invent a toy" and explain to the group later how the toy would work and why it would be useful for play purposes.

People Topics

Objective

To foster growth in the children's awareness of happy feelings as they tell about persons who make them happy

Materials

Pictures of pleasant faces from catalogues, magazines, or posters

Procedure

For this session, cut out pictures of people of various races with pleasant faces. They may be doing different things. Be sure to get both male and female faces from all races. Mount these pictures on small pieces of construction paper. At circle time, place these face up in the center of the circle. Then let the children look at the pictures for a time and choose a picture that gives them a happy feeling. Each can hold up a picture for all to see, and tell how it makes him or her feel.

A variation of the game would be to have the children select their pictures before circle time and hold them face down during the circle. Then as the children take turns telling of their pictures, they hold up their pictures with the faces showing. The children should tell why the face on the picture gives a happy feeling: "It gives me a happy feeling because the person is smiling," or "I like the person in this picture because he looks like my daddy." They can then tell about the person the picture resembles.

In the end, the leader can summarize the children's comments. Close with a comment on how wonderful it is to have persons in our lives who give us happy feelings.

Lesson Extender

After the children have selected pictures of persons they feel give them happy feelings, you could go on to explore further the significant persons in their lives. One way to do this would be to make family booklets for each child. The children could draw pictures of their family members, or write a description of each family member. Preschoolers could dictate their words to an adult who would write them down. Let the children tell what each family member does to help the family. Let the children also describe their brothers, sisters, and others who live in the home.

An especially intriguing exercise is to have the children make up a story about their families, or to relate an anecdote from actual family experience. The children could also be encouraged to bring in pictures from home, or artifacts that represent home to them. It is important to receive the children's comments graciously —whether positive or negative—about their families.

Another approach would be to have the children make up fantasy stories about what they would like special persons in their lives to do. They could plan an imaginary trip or other outing. They might also plan an outing that the family could actually go on. The point is to get children to become more aware of persons in their lives and of their own relationship to these persons.

ॐ

Kind Deeds
That Give Happy Feelings

Objective
To stimulate the children's recall of something that someone did for them that gave them happy feelings

Materials
None

Procedure
Explain to the children that they are going to recall times that give happy feelings. The teacher should begin with his or her own incident— something simple so that the children will be at ease to remember similar events. Perhaps you can tell about a time when a child helped carry your books, or a time when a family member brought you breakfast in bed.

Then invite the children to tell about something that someone did to them that made them happy. (The fact that the happy feelings come from doing things for others will be a topic in the companion volume, *37 Activities for Developing Concern for Others*.) Encourage the children to speak one at a time, and to listen to one another, because at the end they will try to remember what everyone has said. Let the children each have a turn to talk, not going around the circle in order, but with each child speaking when he or she feels ready to. When all who wish to have spoken, restate briefly what each has said, or let one child help remember what everyone has said.

Conclude the session with a statement such as: "Today we have remembered times when we were happy because someone had done something kind for us. We have put all our happy feelings together so that we are really filled with happy feelings. Thank you, boys and girls."

Lesson Extender

Children may extend this session by writing down lists of kind deeds that others have done for them. The list should be long, if the children think of the many incidents, though small, that have happened at school and home. Children tend to tell of the misfortunes, or unfair treatment of others, and that, too, should be discussed at a later session. But the purpose of this session is to build appreciation for little deeds of kindness that tend to be overlooked.

If the children cannot think of many kind deeds that have been done for them, you stimulate their thought by telling of many incidental kind deeds that have been done for you, recently or when you were a child. Also, remind the children of the services rendered to them by such persons as the custodian, the school cafeteria workers and cleaning persons. Perhaps you could have the children write thank you notes to such persons, mentioning specific deeds that they have done which the children have noticed.

Thank you notes to parents, relatives, friends, siblings would also be a good project for the children to pursue.

è&

Places That Give Happy Feelings

Objective

To enable the children to further develop their awareness of happy feelings, centering attention on special places

Materials

A paper for each child, pencils, crayons

Procedure

Invite the children into the circle, and tell that they are going to have fun remembering special places. Remind them that each person has some favorite place—someplace that we remember because we had happy times there. Give some simple example from your own experience. For instance, you might say: "In our back yard, we have a large maple tree, and in the summer it is nice and shady under the tree. We have named the tree Big Tree and my whole family often sits on a blanket under it in the summer and eats a picnic lunch. So when I think of a happy place, I think of that grassy spot under Big Tree. It really gives me a feeling of happiness. Now perhaps you can think of a place you remember that gives you happy feelings."

Allow time for the children to think, and let them raise their hands and one at a time tell of their remembered place, and the happy feelings it brings. When this was done with four-year olds at the University Child Development Center, the children remembered the following places: "My grandmother's house," "the zoo," "Jackson Park," "our swimming pool." Encourage children to list a variety of happy places. Then summarize by remembering what each child has said, letting one child help you remember.

Dismiss the children with a summary phrase such as: "We have really remembered a lot of places that give happy feelings. It really makes us feel happy all over to think of all these special places. Thank you, girls and boys."

Lesson Extender

Have each child draw a picture of his or her "favorite place," then have the children talk about their pictures. Finally, staple the pictures together to make a book of Our Happy Places.

The children could make a class book of favorite places, or individual booklets. There could be stories, or poems, or descriptive paragraphs written about these favorite places.

Talk about how nice it is to have a place "all your own" where you can go and enjoy being quiet for a while. Talk about places that are special because you return to them from time to time, such as a cabin by the river or grandmother's house.

Then remind the children that in houses of worship, there are always special places such as the altar in a church or the ark in a synagogue. These places have been set aside for important times in worship, to remind the people of God's care for them.

?❧

Animals That Give Happy Feelings

Objective

To foster the children's growth in awareness of happy feelings, by discovering the delight of animals in their lives

Materials

Animal pictures, paper and crayons

Procedure

This session is a celebration of the way animals enrich human lives. As the children tell of animals that give happy feelings, they are extending appreciation, awareness, and enthusiasm for the animal world.

Tell the children that they will again recall happy feelings, only today they will talk about animals that make us happy. Ask them to think about an animal they know—a dog, a cat, a guinea pig, a gerbil, or any other animal, large or small. Then ask if any child wants to begin talking about it. If no one volunteers, you might tell of an animal in your life. For instance, you might say: "At our home we have a little black and white dog named Muffin. She is so small she only weighs four pounds. She is about this long (measure fifteen inches between your hands) and she has a tail about this long (measure six inches). She has beautiful brown eyes and little pointed ears that perk up whenever she hears someone coming. She is so glad to see us when we come home that she jumps all around, and when we sit down she jumps into our laps and licks us. We really love Muffin, and it makes me happy just to think about her."

Then ask if any child can tell about an animal that gives him or her happy feelings. Let the children speak one at a time, as they feel ready. If one child keeps giving more and more examples, suggest that he or she let another have a turn, and come back to that child later.

To add interest and to encourage conversation, have one or a few small, caged animals in class, perhaps at feeding time.

Sometimes there will be sad times recalled because a child will recall an animal that has died. Accept their memories gratefully and explain:

"We have happy thoughts when we remember an animal we loved, and sad thoughts knowing we will not see that animal again. Sometimes happy thoughts and sad thoughts come to us at the same time, and that is all right."

Have a child help you summarize what everyone has said, and dismiss on a note of appreciation.

Lesson Extender

Give each child a piece of paper and a pencil and suggest that they draw pictures of animals that give happy feelings, or farm animals, even imaginary ones, with Playdough. Then let them talk about their pictures or "statues." You might staple the pictures together to form a booklet. If you have pictures of animals cut from magazines, it would be good to have the children sort the pictures into categories of "Farm Animals," "Zoo Animals," "Pet Animals," and "Forest Animals." Of course, some animals will fit more than one category, but let the children explain their reasons for the stacks or categories into which they place each animal.

Stories about animals are abundant in libraries, and could be read to the children. If it is a story about talking animals, let the children discuss why it is a "make-believe" story instead of a scientific account. Such a separation should not take the fun away from animal discussion, but should actually liberate the children to enjoy fantasy without the threat of something happening in their own lives such as happened to "Little Red Riding Hood."

Older children could play "Twenty Questions," in which each child thinks of one animal and the other children ask questions that can be answered with yes or no. The object is to guess what animal is in mind in less than twenty questions. The children take turns having the secret animal in mind.

ह•

Something I Made with My Hands That Gives Me a Happy Feeling

Objective

To help the children realize the joy that comes from creativity, and to express their own creative experiences

Materials

Pipe cleaners, scissors

Procedure

To provide numerous experiences in the joy of creativity, a series of experiences could be planned.

Give each child four pipe cleaners. Tell them that a person can put pipe cleaners together many ways and make little persons or animals. The pipe cleaners can be bent, twisted together, or cut different lengths with scissors. You might show an example of a "stick figure," but urge the students to make their own creations. As they work, let them talk about what they are making. Suggest that they also tell of other things they have made with their hands.

Have they ever made a pot out of clay? Have they ever made a doll out of a clothespin? A Halloween "ghost" out of facial tissues? Perhaps some of them have done woodworking. It is a pleasure to use bits of wood, hammer, and nails creatively. A person can take wood chips left over at a lumber mill and glue them together to make something. The children could paint their creations afterwards. Let the children talk as they work, remembering all the things they have made with their hands.

Then ask how it feels to know you can really make something interesting and valuable. Help them see that there is a deep joy in the creative process.

Lesson Extender

Try "box sculpture." For this you merely need empty boxes, such as toothpaste boxes, cereal boxes, detergent boxes. The children each get about six boxes to glue together to make "their thing." Then talk about the joy of creating, and the happy feeling one gets from making something. For small children, the creations are non-representational—that is, they do not necessarily resemble anything. Older children may attempt to make a "house" or a "car." The same joy of creativity is there whether the product is abstract or representational.

The children could make clothespin dolls from the one-piece clothespins, by adding pipe cleaner arms and bits of cloth for clothing. They could make boats of styrofoam trays and dowel-stick masts, with paper sails. They could make binoculars by gluing together two empty cardboard toilet tissue rolls. The idea is to set the stage for creativity, and then let the children talk about happy feelings that come from "something I made with my hands."

ૐ

Happy and Sad Feelings

Objective

To enable the children to distinguish between happy and sad times, in an increased awareness of feelings

Materials

A large piece of paper, 12" x 18", or tan construction paper. On one side of the paper, there is a large circle, with a smile face marked in it; on the other side there is a large circle with a frown face. Black felt markers make good bold lines for this drawing. Or have a 3" x 5" card for each child, with the smile face on one side and frown face on the other.

Procedure

Children need much practice in identifying feelings. Feelings are as much a part of them as hands and feet, but are much less obvious and therefore more in need of clarification. We list a number of related exercises to help promote awareness. Remind the children that when they were talking about happy feelings recently they also mentioned some sad feelings. When we remembered one dog we were happy to think about, we were sad to know that the dog died. (If a child has told about his pet that died, refer to that child's statement so that the children will have a specific example from their own words.)

Explain to the children that they are going to talk about both happy and sad memories. When they tell of a happy one, show the smile face, but when they tell of a sad one, show the sad face. In this way they will see how each person has both happy and sad times to talk about.

Let the children tell about their own events or instances, or give your own examples if they need you to "prime the pump." If you start the discussion with your own, pick a simple instance where there is mixed feeling and show both sides of the page as you talk. For instance you might tell of a class of children you taught, and how much you loved them (show smile face) and how you moved out of town at the end of the year and had to say goodbye to them (sad face).

Let the children tell of their experiences, and show the appropriate side of your picture for each statement. End by summarizing with the help of a child. Remind them that in life we all have both sad and happy feelings (show picture for this final summary, ending on the happy side) and that's what makes life interesting!

Lesson Extender

Have a number of faces cut from magazines. Give each child a face, be it happy or sad, and let each child tell a story of why the person in the picture is happy or sad. Children could write their stories if they are advanced enough, or tell the stories to the group. It reinforces learning to let the children tell their stories into a tape recorder and then play the recording back to the small group.

Paper plates are good for making happy and sad faces. Give each child a paper plate and a dark crayon. Let each child make a happy face on one side of the paper plate, and a sad face on the other side. Let the children sit two by two, facing each other, and tell stories, using the paper plate to express the happy and sad parts of the story. By using only one plate per child, the idea is emphasized that the same person who is happy one moment may be sad the next, and vice versa.

If there are enough pictures of faces cut from catalogues, you could let the children make "feeling collages" by pasting pictures of people with differing expressions entirely covering a paper. One classroom mural of faces (giant collage) might be more useful than each child's individual collage because it could be put on a wall or bulletin board for permanent display.

❧

Something That Used to Scare Me

Objective

To bring the children to an objective realization of the emotion of fear and to enable them to talk about past fears in a way that sorts fantasy from reality

Materials

None

Procedure

As soon as the children gather in the circle, ask if they can remember a time when they were frightened by something in a story or a television program. Recall with them some of the notions that frightened you as a young child, such as giants in fairy tales or evil characters in television cartoons.

Invite the children to talk about what frightened them. Keep the conversation centered on fears that can be outgrown, fears based on an imaginary, fictional world. Explain that there are many things we fear when we are small that we do not need to fear today.

Incidents from real life will inevitably be mentioned. Accept these incidents warmly, with comments such as: "Yes, it is frightening to be out in a storm. Our fear is good because it tells us to go to a safe place. Tomorrow we will talk more about fear of real things. Today we want to remember the fears that we outgrow as we get older."

It is important to accept each child's statement with no "put down" or squelch. Even if a child gives an obviously silly answer such as, "I get afraid when I see men from Mars coming after me," you can reply with acceptance. For instance you could answer, "It is frightening to imagine meeting persons from outer space." In this way, you are accepting the child's statement without letting the conversation degenerate in any way.

When each child has given an example—or each child who wishes to speak has spoken—summarize what has been said, letting one or two children help you remember. Then conclude with a remark such as: "We have talked about what frightened us when we were younger, and today it is good to know that we do not need to keep those old fears. Tomorrow we will talk about fears that we have today, some of which really help us to seek safety."

Lesson Extender

Children need to realize that everybody becomes afraid at some time or other, and it is therapeutic to talk about fears in order to express rather than repress them. A good book to read with small children is *Where the Wild Things Are* by Maurice Sendak (New York: Harper & Row, 1963). This book is an artistic way of dealing with feelings, and the healthy part of it is that the little boy is in control of his own "raging monsters" at the end of the book. Just as Halloween is a time for releasing fears by "play-acting them," so a certain amount of dealing with fears can be healthy, as long as it is not too frightening.

Keeping in the mood of "make believe," you could let the children draw pictures of the fears they had when younger, to laugh at the unreal creatures they used to fear. An effective way of making "spooky pictures" is to use "crayon resist." The child draws the picture such as a Halloween scene with crayons, and then washes over the picture with a large brush and thin paint, such as thin blue tempera or thin black tempera. The crayoned areas will resist the paint, and will stand out against the blue or black background.

Let each child have a construction-paper pumpkin face, with a smiling face on one side and a fearful face on the other. As each child talks, let the other children turn the smile face up if the story is happy, or the fearful face up if the story is scarey. In this way the children participate in listening and recording the feelings they are hearing.

It is important for the children to realize the universality of fears, and to begin to separate real from imaginary ones. By bringing fears out into the open, we dispel the "fear of fear."

Sometimes It's Good to Be Afraid

Objective
To bring the children to a point where they can sort out fears, in order to distinguish the healthy ones from the ones they do not need to harbor

Materials
None

Procedure
Begin by recalling with the children that in the previous session they discussed what scared them as smaller children. In this session they are going to talk about what frightens them now. Explain that fear is good when it causes us to be alert and to seek safety. "For instance," you can say, "it's a good idea to be afraid of a busy street. If we were not afraid, we might just walk right out in front of a car or a truck. To be afraid can help us to act with safety. But once we have gotten to a safe place, then we do not need to be afraid any more."

Invite the children to mention their own fears. Be open to their ideas. Help them to understand that everybody has fears, and that some fears are really healthy. Suggest, also, that it helps to talk about fears because we see that everybody has some. Try to keep the conversation on the subject, for children will inevitably bring in unrelated ideas. When this happens, gently steer the conversation back on target with words such as: "That's interesting, Sammy, and perhaps we can plan another session on that topic, or we can talk about it more at recess. For now, let's remember some more things that frighten us today."

After the children have finished speaking—usually after each has had one or two turns (avoid one child giving too many examples, so that the attention span of the other children is not lost)—suggest that it is time to summarize what has been said. After the summary, conclude with remarks such as: "We have really talked about a lot of scarey ideas, and we have found that some fears help us find safety, and that some things that we used to fear are no longer frightening. It's good that we can share our ideas about this important topic. Thank you, friends!"

Lesson Extender

Discuss what a person can do when there is a real reason to be afraid. In the following list, there are examples of real fears and imaginary fears. Remember that in a sense all fear is real; if a child fears a goblin or a unicorn, that fear is real. The point here is whether the *object* of fear, that which is feared, is real or imaginary. Read the list slowly with the boys and girls, and let them vote on whether each fear is real or "make believe." Then go back over the list to discuss how one could find safety in the cases of the real fears.

Fear List

Real	Imaginary	
___	___	You have been watching television and you think Frankenstein is going to come to your house.
___	___	You are on a camping trip and you see a snake.
___	___	You are in the house by yourself and you smell smoke.
___	___	You are looking at the sky through the trees and the limbs look like a witch on a broomstick.
___	___	Just as you start to cross a street, the light changes and the traffic begins to move fast in front of you.
___	___	You are playing in the park and you hear thunder.
___	___	You pass a cemetery and you think you see a ghost on a tombstone.
___	___	You look out your window at night and wonder if there could be a giant out there.
___	___	You are walking down a steep hill and you are afraid you might fall to the bottom of the hill.
___	___	You are playing close to the baseball field and are afraid the baseball might hit you.
___	___	You climbed a tree to rescue a kitten and are afraid you will fall trying to get down out of the tree.

୬

Scarey Dreams, Happy Dreams, Funny Dreams

Objective

To help the children realize that everybody has dreams, and that some dreams are frightening and other dreams are happy or funny. They will show this realization by recalling and talking about some of their dreams.

Materials

None

Procedure

Begin this session by telling a dream you have had. Introduce your narration with words such as: "Boys and girls, today we are going to think together about some of the dreams we have at night when we are sleeping. Everybody has dreams, but most of the time we forget them as soon as we wake up. Sometimes, however, we do remember our dreams. If we had a scarey dream we can tell about it and be glad it was only a dream, and not real at all. Then again, if it was a happy dream we can tell about it and enjoy it, even though it was only a dream.

"Last night I had a happy dream, but it was also a funny dream because it was something that would be impossible. I dreamed that all my sisters and their children came to see me (that was the happy part) and we all visited on our front porch, and ate pizza. Well, our front porch has room for about six people on it, and there are more than twenty in my sisters' families, and the problem in the dream was that we couldn't get into the house because I had lost the key. I remember searching everywhere for the key, and feeling embarrassed that we were so crowded on the porch. And I'm not sure where the pizza came from, but when I realized I couldn't find the key I was pretty glad I woke up and found it was only a dream! Wasn't that funny?"

Then invite the children to think hard and remember any dreams they have had, and tell the group about the dreams. When all who wish have had a turn, invite a child to help you summarize. In just a few sentences recall each dream that has been told, and close with summary comments such as: "Wow, we really have told a lot of funny dreams. Isn't it interesting to learn how everybody has dreams, every night? And now if we should have a scarey dream we will wake up unafraid because we know that it was only a dream and such dreams happen to everybody. Let's hope that most of our dreams are happy ones, or funny ones, so we can get a good laugh out of them."

Lesson Extender
Let the children draw pictures of their dreams. They could draw a picture of themselves lying in bed, with the dream drawn as a cloud or as a comic strip balloon, above their heads. They could draw with pencil and crayon, or use pastel colors and rub over the dream to give it a blurred and dream-like quality. Charcoal is also good for drawing dreams, because it can be easily blurred to give it a "dreaminess."

Other good media for expressing dreams are: torn paper pictures, where the children tear bits from different colors of construction paper and put them together like a mosaic; or crayon-resist, as described in suggestions for "Something That Used to Scare Me."

ঈ৯

What Makes Me Angry

Objective
To enable the children to increase their awareness of the emotion of anger and to be able to use words to tell of specific examples or situations that cause this emotion

Materials
None

Procedure
Ask the children into the circle: "Did you ever get really angry?" Explain that everybody gets angry at one time or another, and sometimes it is good to talk about these times. Give an example from your own experience, such as: "It really makes me angry when somebody says 'shut up' to me. If they want me to be quiet, I would much rather that they would ask, 'Please, will you be quiet so I can think?'"

Invite the children to tell what makes them angry. Be careful to steer the conversation toward what, not who, makes one angry. If a child mentions another child's name, suggest that we are not discussing persons, only actions that give angry feelings. It can be hurtful if names are mentioned, especially since children tend to repeat what they have heard others say. If the children are giving similar instances, it is wise to accept their ideas, but lead them on by suggesting that they list as many different anger-causing actions as possible.

Four year olds at the University Child Development Center in St. Louis gave the following list of actions that caused angry feelings:

When somebody pushes your block house over.
When somebody shoves you in line at the water fountain.
When somebody yells at you.
When somebody hits you or pinches you.

When somebody takes the big-wheel you are riding.

When somebody messes up your picture.

When the big kids won't let you play.

Accept each child's statement, with a comment such as "Yes, that really would make you feel angry."

At the conclusion of circle time, summarize the statements. Remark that all of us have angry feelings at times, so we need to be able to talk about our feelings with words, not with fists. When we tell how we feel, the other person is often sorry and there is a good chance that that deed will not happen again.

Lesson Extender

After the group session, let the children sit two-by-two and talk about times they remember when they were angry. Try having the second or third graders sit in threes. Have one person be the "recorder" to write down the comments, one person to be the "interviewed." The interviewer could ask such questions as:

Do you remember the last time you were angry?

Could you tell us about it?

What did you say to the person who made you angry?

What would you say if you had another chance?

Is there any way you might have prevented this situation from happening?

What would you do if something like this happens again?

The object is to help children describe incidents objectively, and become more aware of feelings and causes of feelings. Let the children take turns being the "recorder," the "interviewer," and the "interviewed."

ໂ✿

A Time I Was Jealous

Objective

To enable the children to understand the word jealous and to be able to tell of a time when they felt jealous

Materials

None

Procedure

For this session, there will need to be a word definition. Ask if any of the children know what the word jealous means. If no one can tell the circle, explain that it means wishing to have what someone else has and feeling bad that you don't have it. Then go on to tell of how everybody is jealous sometime or other.

As the circle leader, you will probably need to lead off by giving an incident that you can remember from your life when you were jealous. Sibling rivalry is the greatest cause of jealousy, so perhaps you can remember a time when your brother or sister had something you wanted. Perhaps an older sister or brother was getting privileges that you were still too young to enjoy. Or perhaps a younger brother or sister was getting a lot of attention you would have liked to have had. You might express honestly your feelings that at times you wished you could be that other person, but that you got over your feelings as nice things began happening in your own life.

Then invite the children to tell of any jealous feelings they have had. Be very reassuring that sometimes each of us is jealous. We get over being jealous as happy times come into our own lives.

At this point it would be good to recapitulate the sessions on awareness of feelings. Help the children remember that we have talked about happy feelings, sad feelings, angry feelings, fearful feelings, and jealous feelings. Feelings are as much a part of us as are our hands and feet. We learn to manage our feelings as we learn to manage our hands and feet. But isn't it good to know that all of us have all these feelings, so we are never alone in our feelings?

Close the session by thanking the boys and girls for sharing their feelings with one another.

Lesson Extender

Since the word jealous may be new to some of your students, you may wish to put several definitions of the word on poster paper to place on a bulletin board, as the "new word for the week." You could have the more advanced pupils look the word up in a junior dictionary, and letter the definitions on the poster board. You could play a game of "Jealous is . . ." in which the children comment on what jealousy is to them. They could make a class list, or make individual cartoons similar to the newspaper cartoons that say "Love is...."

Examples of this would be:

Jealous is wishing you had a new coat like your sister's.
Jealous is wishing you could stay up as late as your big brother does.
Jealous is wishing your home were as rich as the homes you see on television.
Jealous is wishing the family paid as much attention to you as to the new baby.
Jealous is wishing you had some new skates like your cousin's.
Jealous is wishing your hair looked like Susy's.

One dictionary definition (*Webster's New World Dictionary*) says that the meaning of "jealous" is "resentfully envious." Thus a jealous person not only wishes he had something belonging to someone else, but actually resents the fact that the other person has it. Let the children discuss their jealous feelings honestly, for the sole purpose of awareness.

❧

A Time I Was Embarrassed

Objective

To help the children learn the meaning of the word "embarrassed" and to enable them to talk about an embarrassing time in their lives, realizing that all people are embarrassed at one time or another

Materials

None

Procedure

Webster's New World Dictionary defines embarrass as "to cause to feel self-conscious." Embarrassment is both an uncomfortable feeling and also a chance that one can laugh at oneself. It is helpful to be able to see the humor in the situation, so that the discomfort is lessened.

After the children have gathered in a circle, explain that you are going to talk about embarrassing situations. Then go on to define the word "embarrassed." First ask the children if they know what that word means. Try to draw out their definition. Suggest that a person is embarrassed when he or she feels very uncomfortable because of a mistake.

Give a simple example from your own life, such as: "When I was in the sixth grade, I was invited to a birthday party. I thought the party was on Tuesday, but it really was on Wednesday. Imagine how embarrassed I was when I rang the doorbell and was standing there with my present in my hand, when the birthday friend came to the door and said, 'Why are you here?' I said I had come to the party, and then my friend said, 'Well, the party's not today, it's tomorrow.' I felt really stupid. I was very uncomfortable because I had made such a ridiculous mistake. But fortunately my friend helped me feel better. She said, 'Wow, you're really a good friend, so eager to come that you come a day early; that's really great. Come in and stay awhile and you can come back tomorrow for the party!' I felt better when she said that, and then we were able to laugh together about my mistake. But I'm glad she didn't laugh while I was still feeling uncomfortable."

Then invite the children to tell of any time they can remember when they were embarrassed. Also let them tell how someone helped them to feel better, so that they could see the humor, and nobody was laughed at. We need to emphasize that it is hurtful to laugh when someone is uncomfortable. Laughter is only for a time when everybody sees the humor and can be jolly about whatever has happened.

When the children have told their embarrassing situations, and you have thought of ways to help the embarrassed person feel better, let a child help you summarize what everyone has said. Close with a "wrap up" statement such as: "We have told of some embarrassing moments today, and it's good to know that none of us is alone in having these uncomfortable feelings. It's also good to hear how people have helped us feel better."

Lesson Extender
Second and third graders might write up an account of a time when they felt embarrassed. Younger children could tell their stories into a tape recorder. Let the children learn to laugh at the humor in the situation without losing sight of the need for sensitivity to help the embarrassed person feel at ease again.

ह

Something Funny Happened

Objective

To lead the children to recognize the value of laughter and to learn to distinguish between laughing *with* and laughing *at* a person

Materials

None

Procedure

Begin by telling the boys and girls that they are going to talk about funny things they have done, and that they are going to have fun laughing together. Explain that when we can laugh, we can feel relieved; and that we feel much better when we can have a sense of humor.

Then tell some funny incident from your life. It could be as simple as the following anecdote:

"One morning I slept too late, and when I woke up I had only ten minutes to get dressed, eat breakfast, and get into my car. In my rush, I grabbed two shoes out of the closet, put them on, and did not bother to look at my feet. After I had gotten into my car and was halfway to school, I looked down at my feet and guess what I noticed! I had on one brown shoe and one black shoe. Isn't that silly? But I did not have time to change my shoes, so I had to go all day wearing one brown shoe and one black shoe. I told the boys and girls in the class where I taught, and we all had a good laugh together."

Then invite the children to tell of any funny things they have done, or that they remember having happened in their lives. Encourage the children to laugh, because we are not laughing at a person, rather we are laughing with a person. Explain that sometimes it is not good to laugh, if we are laughing at a person who is embarrassed or hurting. But to laugh with somebody who is already laughing at himself or herself is both humorous and helpful.

Lesson Extender

The children could tell of funny antics monkeys perform in the zoo, or at something comical on television. Let them sit, two by two, exchanging "funny stories."

An interesting way to arrange the discussions is to have the children sit back to back. Have them tell funny stories without being able to see each other's faces. They will realize how much expression helps convey a messsage. Then let them turn and face each other, turning the chairs completely around, and tell the same funny anecdotes by using facial expressions and gestures, but no words. They will realize how hard it is to communicate without words, but they will get the message across in a different way, and often the situation becomes particularly humorous.

If time permits, the children could draw pictures of the funny incidents, and let other children guess what is happening in the pictures.

略

Review of Feelings

Objective

To enable the children to recognize feelings of happiness, sadness, anger, fear, jealousy, embarrassment, and humor as human emotions, and to describe each emotion in words and actions

Materials

Choose from this list of materials the items you will need for the activity you select as your means of review.

Plan 1: A box with a hole in the lid so a child can reach in; slips of paper with the names of emotions written on them.

Plan 2: Pictures of persons with various facial expressions of emotions.

Plan 3: Paper bags for each child, with crayons or markers. Each bag should be small, just the size to accommodate one hand.

Procedures

Plan 1: Place the slips of papers in the box. Let the children take turns reaching into the box and drawing out a paper. The child then pantomimes the emotion written on the paper and the other children guess the emotion. It is wise to announce ahead of time that the children must raise hands and take turns guessing the emotions. The children can pantomime the emotions of happiness, sadness, anger, fear, etc., merely with facial expressions, if you are limited in space; or they can pantomime the emotions by walking the way a sad person would walk, or a happy person would walk, combining body motions with facial expressions. The latter plan is preferable if there is enough space. Play the game until each child has had a turn.

Plan 2: Show the pictures, one at a time, and have the children guess what feeling that person pictured is showing.

Plan 3: Let the children draw faces on the bottom of the paper bag and give feeling expressions to the faces. Then let the children hold up puppets one at a time and let the children guess what feeling that puppet is having. If time permits, there could be conversations between two puppets telling how they feel and why. This could be done for the whole group, or children could pair off for puppet role play. (*Note:* The easiest way to work the puppets is to have the child's fingers work the botttom of the bag, folded over so that the bottom is the head and the rest of the bag is the body.)

Lesson Extender

For any of these activities, you could add situation examples. To do this, read the following situations, and in *Plan 1* the children could act out appropriate gestures; in *Plan 2* they could choose pictures to match the feelings of the situations; in *Plan 3* they could use puppets to act the situations. In each case, the value is in recognizing the appropriate emotions to match each situation:

1. You have just gotten a birthday present. It is a new puppy, and you always wanted a dog of your own.
2. You have accidentally spilled your milk all over the table.
3. You hear a strange noise in your room at night.
4. Your friend has walked home with another friend and left you to walk alone.
5. A classmate scribbled an ugly mark on your drawing.
6. Someone pushed you as you were standing in line.
7. Your teacher told you that your paper was very good.
8. Your mother told you that you cleaned your room well.
9. A child has knocked over a tower of blocks you were carefully building.
10. Your sister got a new coat because her old one was worn out, but your old coat was not worn out so you do not get one now.
11. Grandmother brought each child in the family a present.
12. You are walking home from school and it begins to thunder and the sky is getting very dark.
13. You knock on your friend's door with a birthday present in your hand, only to learn that the party is not today but tomorrow.
14. It is almost time for the class bell to ring when you discover that you have put on two different socks.
15. Your teacher announces that this week the whole class is going to go on a field trip to the zoo.
16. When you get home from school, you find that your pet hamster has died.
17. On a hot day your family is going swimming.

ès

Isn't It a Wonder?

Objective

To alert the children to wonders around them, and to have them point out and describe some wonders they have seen in nature

Materials

If possible, bring to class a copy of the book *Isn't It a Wonder!* by Carrie Lou Goddard. Or show a video with beautiful nature scenes. For an alternate plan, use items from nature and other decorative items. If these are unavailable, bring in pictures of mountains, oceans, birds, fish, and flowers.

Procedure

If you have the book, read it with the children, and then let the children point out some wonders in the classroom or out the window. If you do not have the book, hold up the pictures or show the video and talk about beautiful places in nature. Your words might be, "Isn't it a wonder how the world has so many beautiful places? Wonders are scenes or items in nature that cause us to marvel at how beautiful they are. A wonder is anything wonderful. It could even be something surprising that happens to us."

Ask the children to tell about any wonders they can remember. If they have trouble at first, ask if they have ever looked at clouds in the sky. If it is a sunny day, it would be good to take the group outdoors and look at the sky and talk about the way the clouds are scattered in little clumps. Clouds are wonders, and sunshine is a wonder, too. Even rain is a wonder, in that it waters the earth and helps flowers and all living things to grow.

Let the children look around them out of doors and notice as many details in nature as posssible. Suggest that each of these details are "wonders." Suggest that they watch for wonders the rest of the day so that you can talk more about these marvelous touches of nature the next time you meet.

It would also be good to have the group make up a poem about something wondrous in nature. You might try a Haiku, which is a three-line description of nature. The first line has five syllables, the second line has seven syllables, and the third line has five. Usually the third line is a sort of punch line with a surprise ending. This poetry form is from Japan and is very popular with persons of all ages. Here is an example of a Haiku:

Daffodil, bright gold,
I see you lift lofty head
Blooming in the snow.

To write a Haiku as a group, select a scene or wonder from nature as your subject. Let the boys and girls tell the circle something about the subject, and write their suggestions on the board. Select your first line from their suggestions counting out five syllables. Let the children count with you. Then select the second line and perhaps rephrase it a bit to have seven syllables. Finally, select a third line with five syllables. Copy the completed poem on the board and compliment the children on their poetic skill. Invite the boys and girls to try writing Haiku poems of their own.

Lesson Extender
Have a box of items from nature for the children to feel and describe. The box could include such things as pine cones, sweet gum burrs, twigs, rocks, gourds, straw, nuts, evergreen sprigs, feathers, and seashells. Let the children take turns closing their eyes, taking an item from the box, and describing how it feels—rough or smooth, hard or soft, heavy or light, etc. They can then guess the name of the item, judging from the way it feels.

Another plan could include the above actions but add another activity. Include among the "wonder" items some that are manufactured such as styrofoam balls, Christmas tree ornaments, ribbon, small bells, and coins. After the children have felt and guessed what the items are, let them sort them into two piles: one for natural wonders and one for manufactured wonders. Sorting is a good learning experience for young children.

ॐ

Wonders That Grow
Out of the Earth

Objective

To heighten the children's awareness of wonders that grow in the ground, and enable them to use words to describe their own findings

Materials

If possible, use open ground for this class session. Each child should have at least four square feet of territory to examine. Large magnifying glasses would be quite helpful. Each child should have a small plastic bag.

Procedure

Take the children to their area of ground, and let them sit on the ground in a large circle. Designate the area around each child as his or her "hunting ground." Suggest that each child search his or her area for interesting items of nature which we will call "wonders." They can notice some items without uprooting them, and they can put some into their bags. Let them use the magnifying glasses, sharing them. Allow about ten minutes for the "search for wonders." Then ask each child to tell the group what he or she has found, and why he or she thinks it is a "wonder."

Share the enthusiasm of the children for each item. Exclaim at the marvelous way the earth brings forth plants—grass and flowers and all kinds of interesting weeds. Try to find an earthworm and tell how helpful these little creatures are in keeping the earth loosened so the roots of the plants can stretch downward and grow. Look for interesting rocks, bugs, or even frogs and turtles if such should be present.

Perhaps you could quote the poem by Robert Louis Stevenson, *The world is so full of a number of things, I'm sure we should all be as happy as kings.* When the children have all had a turn to talk about what they have found, let them return to the classroom, bringing back all that they have collected in their plastic bags. The bags could be pinned to a bulletin board as a reminder of "the day we found the wonders."

Lesson Extender

Another way to explore wonders from the earth is to have a planting session. Give each child a paper cup with some potting soil in it, and some marigold seeds. The children can plant the seeds and water them. Place the cups in a window, or on a window sill. Let the children look each day for the emerging "wonders" and enthuse as they see the plants grow and develop. The children could later take the plants home, or plant them outdoors near the school. If these children stay near the school for the whole summer or fall, they could gather seeds in the fall to save and re-plant, learning of the wonder of the cycles in nature!

Grass seed is also an object of wonder. It can be planted in earth on a window sill. It is even more effective to have the children plant something they can later eat. Plant some radishes or tomatoes in a window box or out of doors, and later make a salad for the children to have at snack time. The wonder of roots, stems, and leaves is truly exciting to behold. Let the children wonder about the parts of the plants they eat: when we eat radishes we are eating roots, when we eat celery, we are eating stems, and when we eat lettuce, we are eating leaves. Children will laughingly ask, "Do you eat roots?" and then answer their question by saying, "Yes, you do, when you eat potatoes!"

Another idea of earth wonders pertains to beans. Place lima beans at the edge of a glass jar, with blotter paper between the beans and the sand in the jar. Moisten the sand. The beans will sprout, and their roots and stems will be clearly visible along the sides of the jar! Wonders are numberless—live them up with the children!

ॐ

Wonders That Swim

Objective

To heighten the children's awareness of underwater wonders and enable them to identify with them in imagination

Materials

If possible, a goldfish bowl should be placed in the center of the circle, so that the children can observe the fish swimming around. If no goldfish bowl is available, another aquarium would serve quite well, even though the group session might need to be held at the site of the tank, since a tank cannot be moved easily. With absence of either of these resources, pictures of fish and underwater life will suffice.

Procedure

Gather the children in a circle and tell that they are going to think together about wonders that abound in the sea. Suggest that the children gaze at the fish, with fins and gills and mouth and eyes to supply all its needs. Talk about the beautiful bright colors of the fish, and let the children tell what they noticed most as they watched the fish swim. Ask the children if they could imagine what it would be like to be a fish.

Then invite the children, one at a time, to try to tell how they think life as a fish would be, talking in the first person. Let them imagine they are a fish, and then tell their story. Children might say such things as: "I am a goldfish. I have a tail and fins. When I swim, I flop my tail and wiggle my fins and I go right through the water."

A book that could accompany this session is Leo Leonni's *Swimmy*. Let the children see how fish often swim "in schools," going everywhere together. Suggest that perhaps later in the day they can draw fish, using wet chalk for a brilliant effect, or "payons," which are crayons designed to be used on wet paper. Or let the children draw fish with crayons and "wash" over the page with thin blue paint to give a marine effect.

The concluding remarks could be to the effect that the sea is full of wonders! Suggest that the children say to themselves during the day, "I am a human part of a wonderful world, in which fish swim and birds fly."

Lesson Extender

There is a *Time Life* filmstrip on underwater creatures that would be a good accompaniment to this session. There is a book, also, on underwater creatures, put out by *Time Life*. It would be good to show pictures of the jellyfish, the shark, etc. Let the children draw pictures of underwater scenes with crayon, and "wash" over the pictures with a crayon-resist technique. Or take a trip to an aquarium.

If your school has access to a pool, it would be excellent to have a swim program for your students. Get as many parents as possible to participate, so that each child has an adult in the water—usually one adult can supervise two or three children. The goal of the program is to give the children experience in the water, getting the feel of it. They learn safety rules, and respect for the water from the safety point of view. They also learn the joy of going in the water together, as a group, to feel the wonder of water. Learning to swim is incidental, but can be an added boon to the program if an adequate staff of swim instructors is provided.

૨&

Wonders That Fly

Objective

To heighten the children's awareness of airborne wonders and enable them to tell in first-person narrative how it might feel to soar through the clouds

Materials

A copy of the book *Jonathan Livingston Seagull* by Richard Bach, or other pictures of birds flying. Also a parakeet cage or canary cage; perhaps a bird house or bird feeder.

Procedure

Gather the children around the cage, if one is handy, and explain that they are going to talk about wonders that fly. Show pictures of the birds, and for older children you might tell the main events of the seagull story, reading a few, short passages. Ask the children if they have ever watched birds in the sky. Invite them to describe any birds they have ever seen.

Then ask if any child would like to volunteer to imagine that he or she is a bird. Ask the child to tell in the first person how it feels to fly through the sky. The child might use words such as: "I am a seagull and I flap my wings and I take off up, up into the sky. I sail along over the clouds and sometimes I go down to the water to catch a fish."

Or ask the children to watch the bird(s) in the cage, and then try to imagine they are the birds. Have children take turns giving first-person descriptions of themselves as birds. Their description might go like this: "I am a canary, and I am yellow. I have two wings and two feet and a yellow beak. I say 'chirp, chirp.'"

Talk about what the birds eat, and how they need water, just as people do. Conclude with a summary of the event, such as, "Isn't it a wonder the way the world is created with so many different and beautiful little creatures! Today we have talked about wonders that fly." Then read what one poet wrote about wonders:

All things bright and beautiful
All creatures great and small
All things wise and wonderful,
The Lord God made them all.

Each little flower that opens,
Each little bird that sings,
He made their glowing colors,
He made their tiny wings.

The purple-headed mountain
The rivers running by,
The sunset and the morning
That brightens up the sky.

The cold wind in the winter
The pleasant summer sun,
The ripe fruits in the garden,
He made them every one.

He gave us eyes to see them,
And lips that we might tell
How great is God Almighty,
Who has made all things well.

Cecil Francis Alexander (1818-1895)

Lesson Extender

A trip to the bird sanctuary of the zoo would be the best way to develop this lesson. Bird books should be in abundance on your browsing shelf.

Also, the children could make papier maché birds. To do this, let them each have three pieces of newspaper (one-quarter the size of a full page). The children roll up the first piece of paper, and place a small rubber band at the "neck." The second piece of paper is dipped in a mixture of flour and water (buttermilk consistency) and rolled around the first piece. This wet piece is then shaped into the body, tail, and head of the bird, with a beak pinched at the end of the head. The body can be quite crude, and should be entirely the child's work. Wings can be added from the third piece of newspaper, if it is dipped in the flour water and folded across the body to look like wings. Let the birds dry near a heat source overnight, or on a window sill if it is summer weather.

The next day, let the children paint the birds bright colors. Then they can glue feathers to the birds. Feathers can be purchased in the hobby department of many stores. For added effect, set a bare tree branch into a Christmas tree stand, and fix the children's birds to the tree with tape. The display is colorful and helps the children interiorize the "wonders that fly!"

ล.

The Wonder of Night

Objective

The children will begin to develop an aesthetic appreciation for great works of art, and to heighten their awareness of the beauty of nighttime

Materials

A picture of *The Starry Night* by Van Gogh, or some other striking night-sky photo

Procedure

Gather the children into a circle and display the picture. Explain that this is a world-famous picture called *The Starry Night* by an artist named Vincent Van Gogh. Have the children repeat his name in unison. Ask the children to spend one minute looking at the picture in silence. Then ask quietly: "Would any of you like to tell us something you see in the picture?" Some of the children will point out details such as the church or the houses. Others may say that they see "fireworks in the sky." Explain that the artist was not trying to copy the sky as a camera would. He was trying to express his excitement about the night sky. Perhaps he knew that every star is really a sun, far, far away. So he painted stars like suns. And he painted swirling patterns to express the way the stars are in motion.

Ask: "How do you think this artist felt about night? Would he have said, 'Oh, I guess it's all right?'" Encourage the children to tell what Vincent Van Gogh would have said about night. You might help them by suggesting a formula such as: "My name is Vincent Van Gogh, and I went outside last night and I saw . . . and I felt. . . " etc. Ask them to describe a starry night they remember.

Suggest to the children that they look out a window at night sometime soon and see their own view of the wonders of nighttime. Then at the following session, ask them to tell how their sky looked. Thank the boys and girls for sharing this experience with you, and tell them that the picture will be kept in view for the next few days.

Lesson Extender

Show the children a globe, and then shine a flashlight on it. Let the children slowly turn the globe, as you hold the flashlight on it so that one half of the globe is lit and the other half is in darkness. The children can then be given to understand that the sun is like the flashlight, and as the earth turns, day is on one side while night is on the side away from the light.

Let the children make "night and day" pictures. Paste a dark piece of construction paper, 9" x 12" on half a light piece of paper 18" x 12". Thus there is a light field and a dark field. Let the children paste pictures on the fields, night scenes on the the dark fields and day activities on the light field. Thus they are reinforcing their awareness of the wonder of daily recurring light and dark, and accompanying activities.

There are many readings you can do with the children to emphasize the wonder of night. Appropriate passages from biblical literature include Genesis 1:3-5; Psalm 136:1-9; Psalm 74:16 (Revised Standard Version). Consult the library for suggested materials you might use to bring out the wonder of night.

❧

The Wonder of Mona Lisa

Objective

To enable the children to continue in sharpening aesthetic appreciation and to be able to respond to another famous painting

Materials

A reproduction of *Mona Lisa* by Leonardo da Vinci

Procedure

Begin with the picture concealed from the children, and ask if any of them viewed the sky last night. Remind them of the painting, *Starry Night*, and briefly discuss any night scenes the children describe. Give warm appreciation for their observations.

Then tell the children that today you have another great painting to view with them, but this painting is not of nature. It is a picture of a person. Then turn the picture so that the children can see it. Suggest that they look at it while you tell its story. Then say: "This is a great painting called *Mona Lisa* by an artist named Leonardo da Vinci. (Have them repeat his name.) He was an Italian artist who lived four hundred years ago. He worked four years painting this picture because he wanted the picture to say something about the deep thoughts and fine personality the lady had. Ever since the painting was finished, people have looked and looked at it because it is a great portrait. Today the original painting is in the Louvre (museum) in Paris, France, but there are many copies like this one for everybody to see. Nobody can know what Mona Lisa was thinking when she had her picture painted, but everybody who looks at the picture wonders. Do you wonder, too?"

Then ask if any boy or girl would guess what Mona Lisa might be thinking. Ask what questions the children would ask her, if Mona Lisa could speak. Ask if Mona Lisa reminds the children of anyone they know. What is that person like? Explain that paintings are often better than photographs because they express the whole personality. Thank the boys and girls for their cooperation and tell them that you will place the picture prominently in the classroom for the rest of the week.

Lesson Extender

The purpose of exposing children to great works of art at an early age is to give them a chance to identify with greatness. They come to feel that they are a part of a rich culture, and this association will become life-long. Teachers who expose children to great works of art, by having a reproduction of a masterpiece in the classroom at all times, do a real service to the children. The pictures should be changed about once a week, so that they do not become ordinary. But from time to time, get out an old favorite painting for the boys and girls to remember. They will greet the picture as an old friend.

Other pictures that are especially good for children are: Vincent Van Gogh's *Sunflowers* and *Portrait of the Artist as a Young Man*. Some of the landscapes by Paul Cezanne are quite "wondrous" for small children. Ballet scenes by Degas, the French impressionist painter, are appealing to children. Many libraries have picture collections that you can borrow for the children to view.

ટ્▲

The Wonder of Music

Objective

To enable the children to transfer aesthetic appreciation from visual to auditory perception, and to identify their feelings with those of a great composer

Materials

A record of Beethoven's Fifth Symphony, first movement, and a record or tape player

Procedure

Explain to the children that in the last two sessions, they met two great works of art, *Starry Night* and *Mona Lisa*. Today they will meet a great work of art that cannot be seen, but can be heard. Explain that the music you will play is the first part of the Fifth Symphony written by a great German composer, Ludwig von Beethoven. (Have them repeat his name in unison.) Then tell them that this has been called the victory symphony because the music sounds triumphant—and stirs up feelings of joy and victory. Tell how during World War II, this music was played by people who longed for the war to be won and over.

It was particularly important for Ludwig von Beethoven to feel a sense of triumph because he was gradually losing his hearing. He would have been very sad if it had not been for his great music. When he was conducting his Ninth Symphony, he could not hear, but he could see the people clapping and he had inner happiness that his music was meaningful and was appreciated.

Suggest that the children think of something they are trying hard to do, such as learning math or learning to read better. Have them feel the way the music says, "You can do it!" Then play the music. After playing the music, ask the children to tell what they thought as they heard it. Thank them for their suggestions, and plan to play the music quietly as they work on their tasks.

Lesson Extender

There are many other great works of music suitable for young children. Felix

Mendelssohn's *Violin Concerto*, and his *Midsummer Night's Dream* are choice examples. Prokofieff's *Peter and the Wolf* is especially suited for children because it not only carries a narrative, but also introduces sounds of the various instruments of the symphony orchestra. Tchaikovsky's *Nutcracker Suite* has many themes delightful for children, and can be most captivating when performed as a ballet. Take time to play these classics for the children. They can be borrowed from a lending library. Then play them softly during "free play" or work times, so that the children continue to experience their wonders.

They can make instruments for a "rhythm band" from salvaged items. For instance "tambourines" can be made from disposable aluminum pie plates, by affixing "jingle bells" bought at a dime store. If you cannot get a pie plate, you can use paper plates. You can make "shakers" from empty detergent bottles filled with pebbles. You can make "scrapers" by stapling sand paper over sections of egg cartons, giving each child two sticks made from dowels. "Chimes" can be nails of varying lengths tied on strings to a coat hanger to be struck with a large nail. Then put a marching record on, such as a piece by John Philip Sousa, and let the children keep time to the music with their rhythm instruments. They could even march, as in a marching band.

The Soap Bubble Experience

Objective

To help the children realize the wonder of their own breath, and what it can produce when given bubble makers, and to use words to describe the bubbles they make

Material

Bubble water and bubble-making rings

Procedure

Give each of the children a container of soapy water and a bubble-making ring. It would be good to play classical music in the background as the children blow the bubbles. Allow about five minutes for the children to blow the bubbles, and then stop the music and ask the children to get ready to put the water and rings away. Allow about a minute for the transition, and then ask the children to raise their hands and tell about the way their bubbles looked. Welcome all conversation pertinent to the blowing of the bubbles. Ask the children to tell about the colors they remember seeing on the bubbles. Ask them to describe how big their bubbles were, and what happened to the bubbles.

At the conclusion of the session, thank the boys and girls for participating so nicely, and remark, "Did you ever realize you could make such beautiful colors and bubbles with your breath? You really made the room beautiful today. You are able to do many things very well!"

❧

I Can Paint with My Breath

Objective
To help the children sense the power of their own breath in creating a work of beauty, and to tell about their experience with a sense of delight and pride

Materials
Several plastic bottles of tempora paint (various colors), drinking straws cut in half to be reduced in length, a few sheets of typewriter paper for each child

Procedure
Tell the children that they are going to experience another wonder! They are going to paint designs with their breath! Then demonstrate this by blowing a few drops of diluted tempora paint across a page. Demonstrate, also, the blowing of a "burst," which will look like a blossom on the "vines" of the other lines you blew. To make a "burst," put a drop of paint on the paper, and hold the straw perpendicular to the paper, with the end of the straw almost touching the food color. Then blow with a "t" sound, as if shooting a pea shooter. The drop will burst into blossom, adding a touch of special wonder to the art work.

It would be good to have their pictures on the floor in the center of the circle as you talk, so that the children can admire their handiwork. Close with an expression of appreciation for the beautiful color designs the children have created, and remark with enthusiasm, "This has really been a delightful experience. Did you ever realize you could paint with your breath? Thank you, boys and girls."

৵

We Can Dance with Balloons

Objective

To give the children an experience in happy feeling, the sense of wonder, and "I can-ness" as they each bat a balloon into the air in time to music and then tell of how it felt to be "balloon dancing"

Materials

An inflated balloon for each child, and recorded rhythmic music such as excerpts from the *Nutcracker Suite* or *Puff, the Magic Dragon*

Procedure

Explain to the children that they will each get a balloon, and that they will be still with their balloon until the music starts. Then each child is to keep batting his or her balloon into the air keeping in time with the music. Suggest that each child touch only his or her balloon, being careful not to bump into any of the other children. Suggest also that they keep their voices quiet during the balloon dance time. When the music stops, each child is to sit in the circle, holding his or her balloon.

With these instructions, the leader will then begin the music as a signal to start the dance. Allow four or five minutes for the dance, and then stop the music and signal children to take their places in the circle. Ask the children how it felt to be balloon dancing. Let them describe the experience.

You may need to collect the balloons when the session is over, so that you can use them with another group. But if you do not need them, let the children take them home.

Close with a joyous affirmation of the children's ability to keep time with the music and engage in balloon dancing.

We Can Dance with Scarves

Objective
To help the children experience beauty in movement, increasing their sense of wonder and of accomplishment

Materials
Strips of thin cloth, about six inches wide and six feet long, or strips of crepe paper about two inches wide and six feet long, recorded rhythmic music

Procedure
Gather the children in a circle where there is enough room to move around, about six square feet per child. Explain that there is an ancient Chinese art of scarf dancing which you believe the children can imitate. It consists of waving the scarf in the air in time to the music. Suggest that each child find a place where he or she won't touch anyone else, and that as the music plays, each child will wave the scarf in the air in time to the music, keeping voices quiet. When the music stops, the children are to return to their places in the circle.

Start the music, and let the scarf dancing begin. When the music is over, and the children are in their places, let them talk about how it felt to be scarf dancing. Tell them how graceful they looked during the dance with their floating scarves.

Gather the scarves and dismiss the children with a note of congratulations on their new accomplishment of scarf dancing!

ये॰

I Can Picture Things in My Mind

Objective

To help the children learn to make mental images, and to use words to describe these images, thereby increasing their sense of wonder and accomplishment

Materials

A potted plant

Procedure

Place the potted plant on the floor in the center of your caring circle. Ask the boys and girls if they ever knew that they could "make pictures in their minds." Explain that they will look at the plant for a minute, with eyes open, and then close their eyes and describe the plant. Suggest that they notice as many parts of the plant as possible, so as to be able to have a good picture in their minds. Then take a minute for everyone to gaze at the plant in silence.

After a minute of silence, suggest that the children close their eyes and raise their hands as each one is ready to describe the plant. The leader will have to keep eyes open to recognize the children as they raise hands. One at a time, the children are to describe the plant as they see it in their minds. React positively to their descriptions, commenting profusely on the importance of their ability to picture the plant in their mind and then to describe it. After they open their eyes, summarize, or have a child summarize, the descriptive details each child has given. Children who are able could even try describing the plant from a "first person" point of view. In this way, a child would say something like: "I am a plant. I have thin green stems and shiny green leaves. I have four pink flowers. I live in a red pot, and my roots are in some very brown dirt."

Once, a third grader, in an exercise of this kind, described the plant in human terms as follows: "I am a plant and I have skinny green arms and big green hands. I have a pink head but I have very dirty feet!"

When the children have finished describing the plant, tell them that great poets and other writers often do something from the mental pictures in their minds. When they see a beautiful sight, they will go home, picture the sight in their mind, and describe what they saw earlier. One famous poem about a field of flowers is *Daffodils* by William Wordsworth. Ask the children if they remember how a daffodil looks. Then read the poem.

> I wandered lonely as a cloud
> That floats on high, o'er vale and hill
> When all at once I saw a crowd
> A host of golden daffodils
> Beside the lake, beneath the trees
> Fluttering and dancing in the breeze.
> Continuous as the stars that shine
> And twinkle on the Milky Way,
> They stretched in never-ending line
> Along the margin of the bay.
> Ten thousand saw I at a glance,
> Tosssing their heads in sprightly dance . . .
> When oft upon the couch I lie
> In vacant or in pensive mood,
> They flash upon my inward eye,
> Which is the bliss of solitude.
> And then my heart with pleasure fills
> And dances with the daffodils.

Lesson Extender

An additional session can be held on the topic of mental images. Follow the same format as above only use a rock as your object. Get a rock about the size of a tennis ball and pass it around for the children to feel. Put it in the center of the circle and have the children look at it in silence for a minute. Then let them close their eyes and describe it.

Making "pictures in the mind" is an exercise that can be done for relaxation in many ways. Children can picture a trip to the beach, in which they describe each detail of the sand, the ocean, the waves, the sea gulls, etc. They can picture lying under their favorite tree in the summer, sitting on a park bench, or lying beside a swimming pool. When they get enough practice picturing things, they can take turns leading the relaxation exercises for the other children.

ટે

Something I Can Do with Crayons

Objective

To enable the children to experience their ability to create something interesting and pleasing by designing a name tag with crayons

Materials

For each child, a piece of construction paper 9" x 12", a few crayons

Procedure

Ask each child to print his or her name in large letters on the paper, and to color a design around the name. The design can be any form the child likes.

Then place the name designs face-up in the center of the circle. Exclaim about all the bright colors you see, the interesting shapes and designs. Then ask the children to think about how wonderful it is that they can do a task such as this. Ask: "Could you do something like this when you were a tiny baby? Could a bird do a design such as you did? A fish? An elephant?" Explain that one of the world's greatest wonders is the ability of human beings to learn and to make beautiful pictures or designs.

Then ask the children to list all the things they can do with crayons. They could make a list something like this:

I can print a name.
I can draw a picture.
I can color a picture.
I can make a sign.
I can make a mural.
I can put crayon pieces on waxed paper and iron them to make "stained glass."
I can paint with melted crayon and Q-tips.
I can draw circles, triangles, squares.

Display the list prominently in the room for the rest of the week to remind the children of all they can do with crayons. Then explain that this is only a crayon list. How big a list could they make if they put down everything they can do in the classroom? Tell them that in the next session you will make that list larger, so that they can think of all the things they can do in a classroom.

Lesson Extender

For the children to build a greater realization of their own abilities, many projects can be done with crayons. We single out crayons as a medium because they are usually available in each classroom.

The lesson mentions using melted crayon with Q-tips. This can be safely done by placing the bits of crayon in the spaces in old muffin tins, and placing the mufffin tins on a warm surface such as an electric "hot plate" on the lowest setting. This project of course needs constant supervision, but it gives striking results, and a sense of pride in the children.

Instruction for using crayons in "crayon resist" can be found in the extension of session *Something That Used to Scare Me*. Other crayon activities are:

Crayon Etching: To do this, have a child cover a surface, such as a square of cardboard with a heavy coating of crayon. Then have the child go over the surface with a different color of crayon. Then have the child scratch through the second surface with a point such as the end of a paper clip (pointed end) to give a contrast in the design.

Ironed Crayon: Scrape bits of crayon shavings from pieces of crayon into a pile, with many colors mixed together. Sprinkle the crayon shavings on waxed paper. Place another waxed paper on top. Go over the waxed paper with a warm iron. The crayons will melt into beautiful colors, giving a stained glass effect. These "windows" can be placed in cardboard frames to resemble stained glass windows.

Crayon Squiggles: Have the children draw circular lines at random on a page with crayons, and then fill in the spaces with various colors. The result is an abstract design with aesthetic beauty, giving a good sense of accomplishment and pride.

❧

Something I Can Do Well at School

Objective

To increase the children's feeling of "I Can-ness" by citing examples of the skills they can perform at school

Materials

Some of the children's past work to remind them of their accomplishments. Perhaps a picture one has painted, a story one has written, or a puzzle one has done correctly. Be sure that there is evidence of each child's accomplishment in your display items. Chalk and chalkboard.

Procedure

Explain that you are going to help the children think of the many tasks they can perform well at school. Tell them that you have a few items to remind them of all that they can do well, but that you want them to tell of other things they can do well. Display each item with a brief comment such as: "Isn't this a really lovely painting? I do like the way the colors flow together here in the center, and the way the lines are curved, almost like a rainbow effect. This is a nice piece of work."

Then remind the children that your display items are only a few of their many fine accomplishments. Ask the children to tell of other things they can do well at school. List their accomplishments prominently. Let each child have a turn or several turns. (Avoid letting the session run too long, beyond the attention span of the children.) At the conclusion, thank the children for all they have said, and express recognition of the fact that if time permitted, the list could be longer. Then have helpers read the list for the group. End with a brief statement such as: "We certainly have listed a lot of our accomplishments, and it gives us a good feeling to realize how many things you can each do well at school."

Lesson Extender

Let the children make a "box movie" of things they can do at school. Get a box at least two feet tall, and two dowel sticks about 1 inch thick for "rollers." Have a roll of shelf paper that will fit in the box. It can be purchased with a 13" or 18" width. Use either width, as long as it fits. Let the children draw pictures of themselves doing school activities, and arrange the pictures along the shelf paper so that they can be seen in the box. Have the children (with your supervision) cut a large square opening in the box where the pictures will show. Then roll the pictures on the dowel sticks and place the sticks through the top and bottom of the box, to the left and to the right of the opening, so that the roll of pictures can be rolled sideways to display one picture at a time. The pictures can be drawn directly on the shelf paper, or they can be drawn on typewriter paper and pasted on the shelf paper. As you roll the dowel stick on one end, the pictures will move across the square opening in the box, like a television screen, showing how many things the children can do at school, and emphasizing the "I Can" feeling.

You could also have a checklist for children to note items they can do. Make it so that most children can check most items such as: write my name, tell my colors, count to ten, separate a square from circles and triangles, show the date on a calendar, take the lunch count to the school office, etc.

ॐ

Something I Can Do Well at Home

Objective

To enhance the children's sense of "I Can-ness" by realizing the many tasks they can do well at home

Materials

A felt marker and a large sheet of paper

Procedure

Explain that today you are going to talk about all the things that the children can do at home that are helpful. Remind the children that they each can do many things at home well, and that these tasks really help the family live better. If they want to start mentioning some tasks they have, let them do so; if not, you can suggest that you will try to remember a few things that you used to do at home. For instance, you remember that you helped your mother dry the silverware, and when you got older, you even washed the dishes.

Then ask the children to tell what they can do at home that is helpful. List the children's statements on the large paper. Have them talk one at a time, and have one or two children help you remember what every child has said. Encourage them to add as many different tasks as possible to the list. They can tell how they help in the kitchen or in their own bedrooms. They can mention how they help cook, and clean, and care for pets. They can tell how they express love, and the happy feelings that come from it.

Accept each statement warmly. If a child gives an obviously silly statement, such as "I can throw my toys all around the room," you can reply carefully, "When we play, our toys do get scattered, but when play is finished we can be a big help at home by picking each toy up and putting it back in its place." Thus you avoid a "put down" of the child and yet you move the action into a positive context.

After each child has had a turn, suggest that your helpers begin the summary of what has been said. Conclude with a remark such as: "Today we have listed the many things we do well at home, and it looks as though you boys and girls are really helpful and capable in your homes. Thank you."

Lesson Extender

In order for the children to come to a realization of their own abilities, it is good to pursue the topic of the activities they are able to perform at home.

One way to increase the children's awareness is to compare what the child can do to what a family pet can do. Let the children make a list of two columns. One column is for the child, one for a pet. Mark these names across the top of each column. Down the sides of the column, list the following activities. Let the child check which he or she can do and which the pet can do.

Activity	I Can Do	My Pet Can Do
Call family members by name		
Sit at table for meals		
Take dishes to kitchen		
Be loveable		
Make up a bed		
Take out the trash		
Come when called		
Draw pictures for decoration		
Make a Mother's Day card		
Visit grandmother when she is sick		
Sweep the sidewalk		
Shovel snow		

Other related activities are: making booklets of pictures and stories of home deeds; making a bulletin board of deeds children can do at home.

❧

I Can Make Rhymes

Objective

To sharpen the children's skills in recognizing rhyming words, and thereby to increase their sense of "I-Can-ness"

Materials

Dr. Seuss' *One Fish, Two Fish, Red Fish, Blue Fish*, or another book abounding in rhymes, chalkboard or easel paper, felt marker

Procedure

Begin by reminding the children that they have been thinking about all the things they can do at home and school. Today they are going to realize something else they can do: make rhymes. Ask the children if they know what a rhyme is. Let them tell all they can about rhyming. Then suggest that they listen to the book you'll read with them, and ask them to think about all the rhymes they will hear. Read Dr. Seuss' book or another book abounding in rhymes. At some point during the reading, ask what words rhyme with specific words. Example: "What rhymes with *fish*?" Let the children think of rhyming words. Continue reading the book, allowing the children to laugh at the amusing pictures and wording.

Then go back and point out some of the funny creatures and ask the children if they can make up names for them. Ask what words rhyme with the made-up names. Give simple words such as "hat" and ask children to list all the rhyming words they can think of. List their words on a chalkboard or on easel paper with a felt marker so the children can see your list. Conclude by reading the list and commenting: "We really have listed a lot of rhyming words. It's good to know how well you can think up rhymes."

Lesson Extender

A feeling of accomplishment can come to children as they make their rhymes into "Quick Couplets." Here are some examples:

Dogs Bark   Squirrels jump
In the park.   Stump to stump.

Rabbits hop   Birds sing
Start and stop.   On the wing.

Owls howl   Horses run
On the prowl.   In the sun.

Get the children started by reading the first line and letting them think up the second line. Or you could read all but the last word and let them guess it.

In addition to rhyming, there is also the fun and accomplishment of alliteration. Alliteration is finding two words that begin with the same sound. Examples are:

happy house   furry fox
busy boy   long ladder
crazy cat   moving mouse
dandy dog   noisy nightingale
elegant elephant   tall tree

Let the children make up examples of alliteration. They can especially have fun finding an adjective that is an alliteration with their own name. Word games give skill and self-confidence!

The "I Can" Song
(to the tune of Three Blind Mice)
    I can read
    I can write.
    See how I draw.
    Hear how I sing.
    There are so many things I can do.
    And every day I learn something new,
    I'm glad to see that you're learning, too.
    We are good.

ﷺ

We Can Write a Poem

Objective
To give the children the experience of tasting success that comes with hearing their own poem read back to them

Materials
A popcorn popper, popcorn, salt, butter, napkins, cooking oil, and a large clean bedsheet, an extension cord

Procedure
Spread the sheet on the floor in the center of the circle. Place the popcorn popper on the sheet, in the center, and connect it to an electric outlet. Place the cooking oil and the popcorn in the popper and gather the children around the circle. Ask them to tell you what they think is going to happen. As soon as it is established that you are going to pop popcorn, explain that something special will happen with the corn. Tell them that you will leave the top off of the popper, and ask what they think will happen. Mention, also, that as this happens, you will write down the words the children say about what they see, what they smell, and what they hear. Explain that their words will make a poem, which will then be read back to them. Ask that they talk one at a time and distinctly so that you can write down their words. Then turn on the popper and wait in silence.

As the first sounds come, ask the children to describe them. Write down their words as they talk. Ask them to tell what they smell, and what they see. Write their words in a list, like a free-verse poem. When the popping is over, let a few children gather the popped corn from the sheet, and put it in a bowl. Add salt and butter, and pass the bowl around for the children to have popcorn to eat. Have them describe how the corn tastes. Add these words to your poem.

When the process is finished, read the words back to the children, so that they can hear their words and realize that they have written a poem. A poem written this way by preschoolers follows:

It rattles when you put it in the pan.
Pop! Pop! It's starting to pop!
Hey, it jumped up high!
Look at it jump!
Wow! Like a firecracker!
I can smell it.
It smells good.
It looks like snow.

There goes another!
And another!
It's funny.
It's playing tricks.
Yum, yum, I want some.
Is it finished?
Can we eat it?
O boy, crunchy.
And salty, too!

Conclude by telling the boys and girls how much you like their poem. Print it on a large paper to display in the room, and also duplicate copies to send home to their parents.

Lesson Extender

If the children enjoyed writing this "free verse," you can introduce them to other forms of poetry. We mentioned writing Haiku poems in the session *Isn't It a Wonder!* Haikus, or another form of verse could be written again with this session. Your third-grade pupils can write limericks, and can feel very good about their accomplishments. To encourage them, start by giving them the first four lines of a limerick and let them make up the fifth. They will come up with some charming lines, and in so doing they will learn the form so that they can create their own entire poems. A limerick has five lines; the first two lines and the last line all rhyme, and the third and the fourth lines also rhyme. There are usually eight syllables in the first, second, and fifth lines, and five syllables in the third and fourth lines. Some limericks have nine syllables in lines one, two, and five, with six syllables in lines three and four. Here is an example:

There was a young lady named Mollie,
Who had a twin sister named Polly.
They both went together,
In all kinds of weather,
'Cause Mollie made Polly feel jolly.

ቈ

I Am Wise

Objective

To enable each child to realize that he or she really knows a great deal and is wise. Children will also practice the skill of making mental images, this time making moving images in the mind.

Materials

A picture of an owl

Procedure

Begin by showing the picture of an owl and asking the children to identify the bird. They will readily respond "owl." Then ask if they have ever heard anything about an owl. For instance, do people think an owl is stupid or wise? Establish the fact that people consider the owl to be wise.

Tell the children that whether they realize it or not, they too are wise. Explain that they will use their imaginations and feel as wise as an owl. Have the children close their eyes, put hands in laps, feet flat on floor, and imagine that they are a wise owl sitting on the limb of a tree. (If the children are sitting on the floor, have them sit with knees out, and feet crossed, under, and hands on knees.)

Give the following guided exercise:

In your imagination, you are a wise owl, and you are sitting on the limb of a tree. Now you decide to fly around and look at the countryside. You unfold your wings and soar from the tree, floating on outstretched wings over the earth below. You fly with ease, and it feels good to glide through the air.

You look down and see a farm, with wheat growing in a field. Over the hill you see the farmhouse, with smoke curling from the chimney. It is night, and the parents and children are sleeping peacefully in the house. You fly over the roadway to the little town nearby and see houses in rows along the streets.

Over at the end of the block there is a store with a big truck parked in the back. And further down the street, there is a church with a tall red steeple. There is a school on the next block, and behind it is the playground with swings and slides. But it is night and no person is in sight. You fly further, and see the fire station with a bright red fire truck. There is an office building next door, and there are cars parked up and down the streets in front of the homes.

You fly back to the countryside again, and glide right back in toward your favorite tree. Refreshed from your night flight, you land back on the limb of a tree, and settle down again to remember all the sights you have seen.

Suggest that the boys and girls gradually open their eyes, and remember what they saw as "owls" flying around the country and town. Let them tell what they remember. Suggest that whenever they feel worried or find it hard to do a lesson, they can remember that they are as wise as an owl. They can remember their imaginary trip, and perhaps repeat softly to themselves, "owl, owl, owl."

Lesson Extender
Children can tell all the ways they are wise like the owl. They cannot fly, but in their minds they can travel anywhere in the world. Let them make a list of all the places they know about, all the people they know, all the songs they can sing, all the books they have read, until they are astounded to realize how much they know.

Perhaps then they could make "owl" badges out of construction paper. Draw the outline of an owl on brown paper and cut it out. On another paper have the children write, "I am wise as an owl." Paste the words across the chest of the owl, and let the children wear their badges home as a reminder of all they have learned.